ULTIMATE
QUESTIONS
&ANSWERS

PLANET EARTH

AUTUMN
PUBLISHING

CONTENTS

WHAT MAKES EARTH UNIQUE?

Earth is the only planet in our Solar System with oxygen in its atmosphere and lots of liquid water on its surface, allowing life, in its various forms, to exist. It is our beautiful blue planet, thriving with a multitude of living animals, plants and, of course, human beings!

Our blue planet

Big? HOW DID EARTH BEGIN?

Scientists think Earth was formed at roughly the same time as the Sun and other planets when the Solar System came together from a giant, rotating cloud of gas and dust known as the solar nebula. As the nebula collapsed because of its gravity, it spun faster and flattened into a disk. Most of the material was pulled toward the center to form the Sun. Gradually, the rest of this vast cloud began to cool and the gas condensed into trillions of droplets. These droplets were slowly pulled together by their own gravity and formed clumps. Leftover particles within the disk collided and stuck together to form other larger bodies, including Earth.

Earth's surface cooling

WHAT IS THE SHAPE OF EARTH?

Earth is not quite a perfect sphere. The spinning of the planet causes it to bulge at the equator. Scientists describe Earth's shape as "geoid," which, interestingly, means "Earth-shaped"!

WHAT DID EARLY EARTH LOOK LIKE?

In the beginning, it was just a fiery ball of molten (liquid) rock. As it cooled, lumps formed on the surface of the molten rock. The surface gradually hardened into a crust. Volcanoes kept pouring steam and gases onto the surface, which led to the formation of the atmosphere. As Earth cooled more, clouds of steam became water, creating enormous oceans. The crust eventually cooled and broke apart to form the continents.

Red-hot molten rock once flowed on Earth's surface.

DOES THE EARTH SPIN AT A TILT?

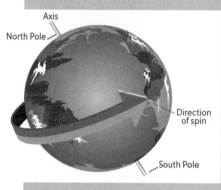

Axis
North Pole
Direction of spin
South Pole

Earth spins on a tilted axis.

Yes, Earth spins around a line between the poles called its axis. The axis is tilted over at 23.5° in relation to the Sun. Earth rotates once every 23 hours, 56 minutes and 4.09 seconds. The Sun therefore appears to come back to the same place in the sky once every 24 hours.

WHY IS THE ATMOSPHERE SO IMPORTANT FOR EARTH?

Clouds are part of Earth's atmosphere.

Wrapped around Earth is a thin blanket of gases, including nitrogen, oxygen, argon, and carbon dioxide. This blanket is called the atmosphere; its thickness is about 60 miles. Yet without it, Earth would be as lifeless as the Moon. The atmosphere gives us air to breathe and clean water to drink, as well as protecting us from the Sun's harmful rays, all while keeping us warm with trapped heat.

Rapid-FIRE ?

WHO FIRST REALIZED THAT EARTH GOES AROUND THE SUN?

The Polish astronomer, Nicolaus Copernicus.

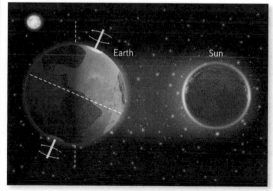

Earth   Sun

A spinning Earth circles the Sun.

HOW FAST DOES EARTH SPIN?

At over 600 miles per hour.

HOW FAST DOES EARTH GO AROUND THE SUN?

At more than 62,000 miles per hour.

WHY DOES EARTH LOOK BLUE FROM SPACE?

Earth is the third planet from the Sun in our Solar System. From a distance, it looks like a great, round, blue jewel hanging in the darkness of space. It is blue because three-quarters of its rocky surface is submerged under blue ocean waters, which shimmer in the light of the Sun.

Clouds swirl above both land and water.

HOW THICK ARE THE PLATES?

There are about seven large plates. Their exact thickness is uncertain, but they could be up to 90 miles deep in places.

Big? WHAT IS EARTH MADE OF?

The structure of Earth can be divided into three parts: the crust, the mantle, and the core. Mostly made up of oxygen and silicon, the crust is the outermost layer. It is the familiar landscape on which we live: rocks, soil, and seabed. Beneath the crust is the mantle, a layer almost 1,865 miles deep. It is made of metal silicates, sulfides, and oxides. This layer is so hot that the rock often flows like sticky street tar—only very, very slowly. Below the mantle is a core of metal, mostly iron, sulfur, and nickel. The outer portion of the core is so very hot that the metal is always molten. The Earth's magnetic field is created here. Earth's inner core is even hotter—estimated to be around 10,800 °F—but the metal is solid because pressure within the inner core is extreme, so the metal cannot melt.

Looking inside Earth

Atmosphere
Mantle
Outer core
Crust
Inner core

WHAT ARE PLATES?

The surface of Earth may appear solid but it is like a giant jigsaw. Earth's hard outer layers are divided into large blocks called plates that float on a partly molten layer of rocks.

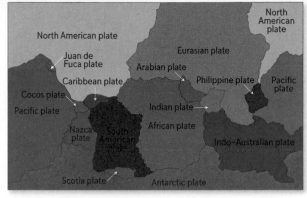

The plates that make up Earth's crust

HOW DO WE KNOW WHAT EARTH'S INSIDES LOOK LIKE?

Scientists have figured this out from the vibrations from earthquakes and underground explosions. This data is pictured with lines on 3D maps to help scientists understand the structure of Earth's core.

Earth's structure

WHAT HAPPENS WHEN PLATES COLLIDE?

Plates move at an average of between one to two inches in a year. If plates collide along a deep trench beneath an ocean, one plate is pulled beneath another and melts and is recycled. On land, when continents collide, their edges are pushed up into new mountain ranges.

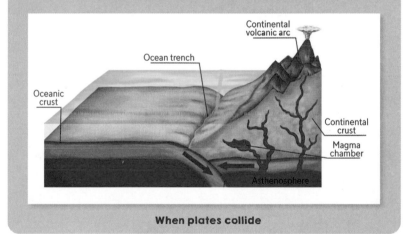

When plates collide

Rapid-FIRE?

HOW THICK IS EARTH'S CRUST?

It varies from 4 to 7 miles under the oceans, to 15 to 43 miles under the continents.

HOW DOES EARTH GET ITS MAGNETIC FIELD?

It is formed in the outer core.

Earth's magnetic field

WHY IS THE CORE OF EARTH MADE OF IRON?

Because as Earth cooled, dense metal like iron sank to the center, while lighter rock-forming materials floated to the top.

WHAT IS EARTH'S ATMOSPHERE MADE UP OF?

Covering the surface of Earth like a thin blanket is a layer of gases that forms the atmosphere. It is made up of 78 percent nitrogen, 21 percent oxygen, and 0.04 percent carbon dioxide. The minute, remaining percentage is made of some other gases, water vapor, and dust. We barely notice this all-enveloping atmosphere, but without it, Earth would be as lifeless as the Moon.

Earth's atmosphere

Rapid-FIRE ?

A barometer

WHAT IS **AIR PRESSURE?**
The weight of air on a surface on Earth. It is measured with a barometer.

WHAT IS THE **IONOSPHERE?**
It is another layer, overlapping the mesosphere, thermosphere, and exosphere, where radio waves are reflected.

A satellite in orbit

IN WHAT LAYER OF THE ATMOSPHERE DO SATELLITES ORBIT EARTH?
The thermosphere.

WHERE IS THE TROPOSPHERE THE THINNEST?
At the North and South Poles.

HOW **COLD IS THE ATMOSPHERE?**

The atmosphere, with all its layers, extends up to 6,200 miles from Earth's surface. Temperatures vary in the different layers: the mesosphere can go down to -130 °F, the exosphere much, much lower, whereas the thermosphere can be as hot as 3,600 °F!

Big? IS THE ATMOSPHERE BUILT UP IN LAYERS?

Exosphere (435 to 6,200 miles) — Satellite

Thermosphere (50 to 435 miles) — Spacecraft

Mesosphere (31 to 50 miles) — Meteors

Stratosphere (7 to 31 miles) — Radiosonde

Troposphere (0 to 7.5 miles) — Clouds

The atmosphere in layers

Yes, the atmosphere has five layers. The lowest layer, closest to the surface of the Earth, is the troposphere. This is where weather is made, and most of the atmosphere's gases are concentrated in it. Above it is the stratosphere. No winds blow in this layer, nor are there any clouds. Beyond it lies the cold mesosphere, with very few gases. It is followed by the thermosphere, the largest and hottest layer of the atmosphere, and lastly, the exosphere, on the edge of outer space.

WHY IS THE STRATOSPHERE VITAL?

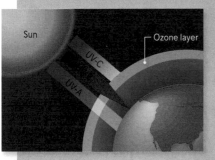

Sun — Ozone layer
UV-C
UV-A

How the ozone layer protects Earth

The stratosphere has a layer of ozone gas, which acts like a thick umbrella covering the layers beneath. By absorbing most of the harmful UV radiation from the Sun, the ozone layer prevents it from reaching the surface of the Earth, enabling the survival of life on the planet.

Precipitation

WHAT IS THE DIFFERENCE BETWEEN RAIN AND PRECIPITATION?

When a lot of water vapor fills the air, it begins to change and condense into droplets of water. These droplets fall back onto Earth as precipitation, which can take many forms—rain, hail, snow, sleet, fog, dew. Rain is just one form of precipitation.

WHAT IS HUMIDITY?

When water evaporates it forms the gaseous water vapor. The amount of water vapor in the air at any one time is known as its humidity. As more and more water vapor saturates the air, humidity increases, eventually resulting in rain, fog, or mist, depending on the heat and temperature of the place.

WHAT ARE LATITUDE AND LONGITUDE?

Every place on Earth's surface can be pinpointed by two figures: its latitude and its longitude. Lines of latitude (called "parallels") form rings around Earth, parallel to the equator. A place's latitude is given in degrees (°) north or south of the equator, which is considered latitude 0°. On the other hand, lines of longitude (called "meridians") run around Earth from north to south, dividing the world up like the segments of an orange. A place's longitude is given as degrees west or east of the prime meridian, which is longitude 0°. Of course, all these lines are imaginary—they exist only on paper.

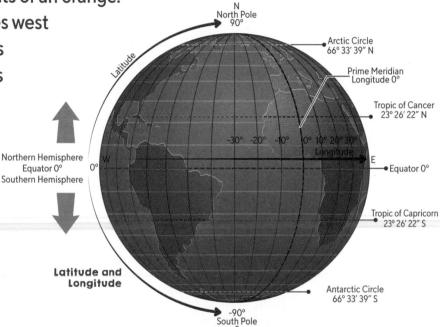

N
North Pole
90°

Latitude

Arctic Circle
66° 33′ 39″ N

Prime Meridian
Longitude 0°

Tropic of Cancer
23° 26′ 22″ N

-30° -20° -10° 0° 10° 20° 30°
Longitude

Northern Hemisphere
Equator 0°
Southern Hemisphere

0°   W   E

Equator 0°

Tropic of Capricorn
23° 26′ 22″ S

Latitude and Longitude

Antarctic Circle
66° 33′ 39″ S

-90°
South Pole
S

Big? WHAT ARE TIME ZONES?

As Earth spins, different parts of its surface turn toward the Sun at different times—the Sun is always rising in one place and setting in another, so, the time of day varies around the world. When it's dawn where you live, it's sunset on the other side of the world. To make it easier to set clocks, the world is split into 24 time zones, one for each hour of the day. As you go east around the world, you put clocks forward by one hour for each zone until you reach an imaginary line called the International Date Line. If you go farther on across the Date Line, you continue adding hours, but put the calendar back by a day.

World time zones

NEW YORK   LONDON   MOSCOW

BEIJING   TOKYO   SYDNEY

WHAT IS THE PRIME MERIDIAN?

This is an imaginary line of 0° longitude that is perpendicular to the equator, and parallel to the axis. It passes through Greenwich in the UK, and divides Earth into eastern and western hemispheres. As it crosses the poles to the opposite side of the globe, the line becomes 180° longitude and is also known as the International Date Line.

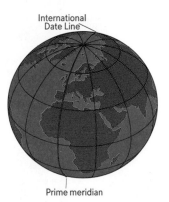

The prime meridian and the International Date Line

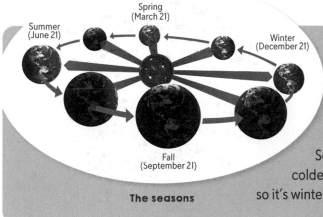

Spring (March 21)
Summer (June 21)
Winter (December 21)
Fall (September 21)

The seasons

WHAT MAKES THE SEASONS?

Earth is always tilted in the same direction as it orbits the Sun. So when Earth is on one side of the Sun, the Northern Hemisphere is tilted closer toward the Sun, making it warmer. At the same time, the Southern Hemisphere is tilted away from the Sun, and is, therefore, colder. When Earth reaches the other side of the Sun, it is the opposite, so it's winter in the Northern Hemisphere and summer in the Southern.

WHAT IS THE EQUATOR?

The equator Is the circle that goes around the center of Earth. It is perpendicular to the axis and divides the planet into two equal hemispheres (or half spheres), the Northern and the Southern.

WHY ARE LATITUDE AND LONGITUDE IMPORTANT?

Two points on Earth can lie at the same latitude but still be far away from each other. Similarly, two distant points may lie on the same longitude. But only one point lies on a particular combination of latitude and longitude. So latitudes and longitudes are necessary for locating an exact point on Earth.

Rapid-FIRE ?

WHERE IS THE ARCTIC CIRCLE?

In the Northern Hemisphere, at 66½° N latitude.

WHERE IS THE ANTARCTIC CIRCLE?

In the Southern Hemisphere, at 66½° S latitude.

Antarctic Circle

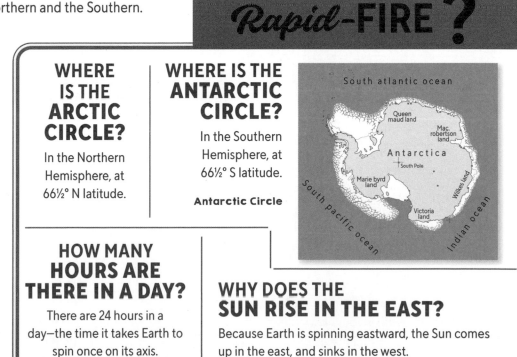

HOW MANY HOURS ARE THERE IN A DAY?

There are 24 hours in a day—the time it takes Earth to spin once on its axis.

WHY DOES THE SUN RISE IN THE EAST?

Because Earth is spinning eastward, the Sun comes up in the east, and sinks in the west.

WHAT IS THE TIME LINE OF LIFE ON EARTH?

Just as the day is divided into hours, minutes, and seconds, geologists divide Earth's history into time periods. The longest divisions are eons, which are billions of years long; the shortest are chrons, a few thousand years long. In between are eras, periods, epochs, and ages. Scientists divide the last 590 million years into three eras: the Paleozoic (meaning "old life"), Mesozoic ("middle life"), and Cenozoic ("new life").

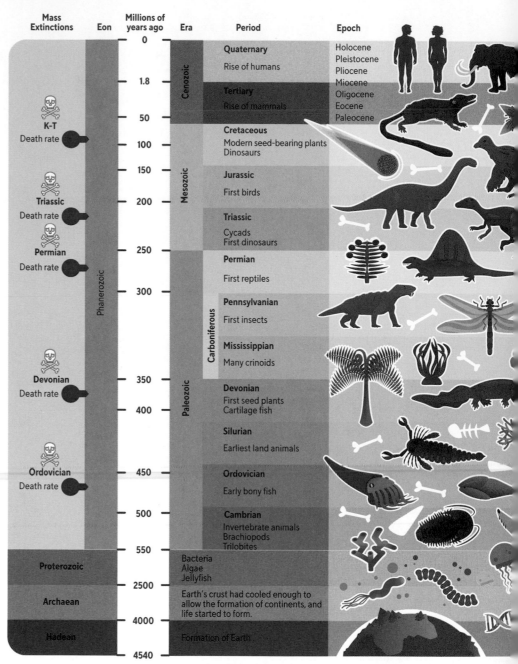

Mass Extinctions	Eon	Millions of years ago	Era	Period	Epoch
		0	Cenozoic	**Quaternary** Rise of humans	Holocene Pleistocene Pliocene Miocene
		1.8		**Tertiary** Rise of mammals	Oligocene Eocene Paleocene
K-T Death rate		50			
		100	Mesozoic	**Cretaceous** Modern seed-bearing plants Dinosaurs	
		150		**Jurassic** First birds	
Triassic Death rate	Phanerozoic	200		**Triassic** Cycads First dinosaurs	
Permian Death rate		250		**Permian** First reptiles	
		300	Paleozoic / Carboniferous	**Pennsylvanian** First insects	
				Mississippian Many crinoids	
Devonian Death rate		350		**Devonian** First seed plants Cartilage fish	
		400		**Silurian** Earliest land animals	
Ordovician Death rate		450		**Ordovician** Early bony fish	
		500		**Cambrian** Invertebrate animals Brachiopods Trilobites	
	Proterozoic	550		Bacteria Algae Jellyfish	
	Archaean	2500		Earth's crust had cooled enough to allow the formation of continents, and life started to form.	
	Hadean	4000		Formation of Earth	
		4540			

Geologic time line

WHAT DID EARLY ANIMALS LOOK LIKE?

By around 500 million years ago, bacteria in the oceans had evolved into the earliest fish. These strange creatures had no jaws; they had funnel-like sucking mouths.

WHEN DID PLANTS START TO GROW ON LAND?

The first land plants appeared during the Silurian period, around 440 million years ago. These simple plants reproduced by releasing spores. Plants produced oxygen and provided food for the first land animals—amphibians. Amphibians first developed in the Devonian period, 420 million years ago, from fish whose fins evolved into limbs.

WHAT ARE STROMATOLITES?

Primitive life forms may have first appeared on Earth about 3,800 million years ago. These bacteria lived in the oceans and built up solid mats of calcium carbonate, also known as lime. The deposits from the bacteria are known as stromatolites.

Stromatolites

WHY DID IT TAKE SO LONG FOR LIFE TO APPEAR?

Earth's surface was probably molten for many millions of years after its formation. Life did not exist for the first 400–800 million years, and first began in water after the forming of the oceans.

Too hot to support life

Big?
HOW LONG AGO DID LIFE APPEAR?

Ammonite fossil

The first signs of life—probably bacteria—appeared nearly four billion years ago. But animals with shells and bones did not appear until less than 600 million years ago—these were the first living things preserved as fossils. It is mostly with the help of such fossils that geologists have built up a picture of Earth's history since then. Very little is known about the four billion years before this, called the Precambrian period, which makes up more than 85 percent of Earth's history.

Rapid-FIRE?

WHAT IS A WOOLLY MAMMOTH?

A prehistoric mammal, which was the ancestor of the elephant.

Woolly mammoth

WHAT IS A FOSSIL?

Fossils are preserved plant or animal remains or traces of life forms found in Earth's crust, from a past geological age.

Fossil of an early fish

WHAT IS THE STUDY OF FOSSILS CALLED?

Paleontology.

HOW MUCH OF EARTH'S HISTORY HAVE HUMANS BEEN AROUND FOR?

If Earth's history was crammed into a day, humans would appear only at the end, just two seconds before midnight!

WHAT IS EVOLUTION?

Life has existed on Earth for millions of years. Living forms and creatures have inhabited almost all of Earth and over the centuries have changed and transformed from the way they existed in the past. This transformation and modification of features and functions in living beings is called evolution. However, it is believed that a few creatures, like the cockroach and the crocodile, have not changed since the era of dinosaurs.

A cockroach

WHO WAS CHARLES DARWIN?

Charles Darwin was an English scientist who proposed that evolution happened through "natural selection." According to Darwin, the organisms that live are those which have the best traits to survive their environment, and pass on those traits to following generations.

Charles Darwin

Big? WHY DO ANIMALS GO EXTINCT?

Imagining an asteroid impact

Extinction is when an entire population of a particular animal disappears from Earth. Though it sounds drastic, extinctions are quite common in Earth's history. Scientists believe that 99 percent—over five billion species that ever lived—have become extinct since the beginning of life. This could have happened due to lack of food or disastrous events like asteroids hitting Earth. In recent times, the speed at which species are becoming extinct has increased due to human activity.

WHEN DID THE FIRST MAMMAL APPEAR ON EARTH?

The first mammals were small and furred, and resembled rats or shrews. *Megazostrodon* was one of the earliest mammals. Though mammals appeared on Earth about 200 million years ago, they became common only after the extinction of dinosaurs.

Megazostrodon

Rapid-FIRE ?

***Entelognathus primordialis*, the first fossil with a face**

WHICH IS THE OLDEST FISH FOSSIL?

Entelognathus primordialis—419 million years old.

WHAT IS A COELACANTH?

A rarely seen, deep-sea fish that has existed since the time of the dinosaurs.

Coelacanth

WHAT IS SIGNIFICANT ABOUT THE CENOZOIC ERA?

In this period there was a rapid evolution of mammals and flora.

WHICH IS THE OLDEST KNOWN BIG CAT?

The leopardlike *Panthera blytheae*, which roamed the Himalayas six million years ago.

WHY IS THE CAMBRIAN PERIOD IMPORTANT?

The Cambrian period extended from 541 to 485.4 million years ago. It was a time when the Earth was still cold but gradually getting warmer. All pre-Cambrian life was aquatic and soft bodied. But because Cambrian animals had hard body parts, many of the earliest known fossils are from this period.

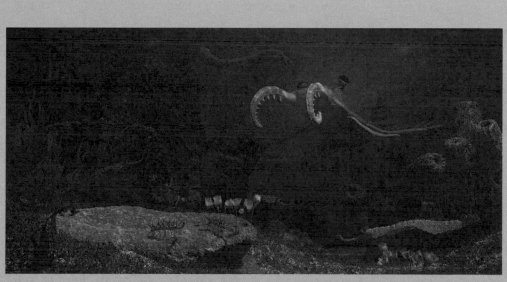

Life in the Cambrian era

WHAT ARE ROCKS?

Rocks are the hard mass which the ground is made from. Though we usually see them exposed in places such as cliffs, mountain crags, and quarries, rocks are everywhere, even deep beneath the ground. Rocks can be as old as Earth itself, and are made of tiny crystals or grains of naturally occurring chemicals called minerals.

Rocky cliffs on a coastline

Big?
HOW MANY TYPES OF ROCKS ARE THERE?

Igneous rock

Sedimentary rock

Metamorphic rock

Sedimentary rock

There are three kinds of rocks: igneous, sedimentary, and metamorphic. Igneous rocks are formed when red-hot magma flows up from Earth's hot core and cools down. Sedimentary rocks form when debris, including plant and organic matter, usually deposited on the seabed in layers, is built up, compressed, and cemented into solid rock over millions of years. Metamorphic rocks are created when movements of Earth's crust or the heat of its magma transforms one kind of rock into another.

WHAT ARE THE MOST COMMON ROCKS?

Sedimentary rocks cover 75 percent of Earth's land surface, but igneous rocks make up 95 percent of the rocks in the top 10 miles of Earth's crust. Though metamorphic rocks are not as predominant, they do make up the largest group of colorful rocks.

WHAT IS THE ROCK CYCLE?

Rocks are continually being recycled to make new rocks in a process called the rock cycle. For example, igneous rocks are gradually worn away by the weather. The weathered fragments are washed down to the ocean and eventually form sedimentary rocks. Similarly, metamorphic rocks can be formed from both igneous and sedimentary rocks.

Rock face eroded by the sea

IS COAL A ROCK?

No. Although coal is sometimes called an organic rock, it is not a true rock since rocks are inorganic (lifeless). Coal is a fossil fuel—like oil and gas—that formed over millions of years from the remains of once-living matter.

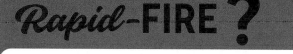

WHAT MAKES LIMESTONE INTERESTING?

It has grains of plant and animal remains, even fossils, embedded in it.

Limestone rock formation

WHAT IS PUDDING STONE?

A mixture of different-sized pebbles cemented by sand, formed in river channels over thousands of years. It looks a bit like a fruitcake.

Pudding stone

WHAT WERE CARBONIFEROUS SWAMPS?

Fossilized fern leaf from the Carboniferous period

About 300 million years ago, in the Carboniferous period, there were huge tropical swamps filled with giant treelike ferns. As the remains of the plants were buried and compacted in these huge, warm swamps, they formed peat. Once they sank deeper, heat and pressure changed the peat into brown coal. Further pressure changed it to black bituminous coal.

WHAT ROCKS ARE COMMONLY USED FOR BUILDINGS?

Limestone, sandstone, and granite.

WHAT ARE MINERALS?

Minerals are natural chemicals from which Earth's crust is formed. There are around 2,000 individual minerals, each with a unique color and shape. A few are powdery or resinous, but most are crystals. Some minerals, such as gold and silver, are pure chemical elements, but the majority are compounds, of which silicates are most common.

Uncut crystals of the gemstone ruby

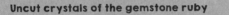

Raw crystals and minerals

Big? ARE GEMS AND CRYSTALS THE SAME?

Crystals are glassy-looking, brittle solids that form shapes with sharp corners and flat sides. Natural crystals form when a liquid cools and hardens, and the molecules in the liquid cluster in a particular pattern—a pyramid, cube, etc. Rare and beautiful crystals such as rubies and emeralds are valued as gems. Many are termed "precious." They are rare because they only form naturally, under very special conditions—usually deep within volcanic rocks.

Crystals of pure quartz

WHAT ARE SILICATES?

When silicon and oxygen, the two most common chemical elements on Earth, combine with a metal, they form a silicate. There are over 500 silicates that exist, and quartz is one.

WHAT ARE VALUABLE MINERALS?

Valuable minerals are either metal or rock that can be processed and converted for economic purposes. Gemstones such as diamonds, rubies, sapphires, and emeralds are valuable minerals. Gold and silver are also precious. Palladium is considered more precious than gold, and it is very valuable to automotive industries.

Palladium

WHAT DO ALL MINERALS HAVE IN COMMON?

All minerals are hard—their resistance to scratches determines the degree of hardness, which is classified from 1 to 10 on the Mohs scale. Talc, calcite, and chalk are soft minerals that sit at the lower end of the scale. Diamond is 10 on the Mohs scale.

Cut and polished diamond

WHY ARE DIAMONDS EXTRAORDINARY?

Very hard, very rare, and very old, diamonds are essentially carbon that has been transformed under great pressure deep inside Earth. It is usually volcanic activity that brings them close to the surface again after billions of years and makes mining possible. Diamonds are the hardest natural substance ever found.

Rapid-FIRE ?

Fluorite crystals

WHAT IS FLUORITE?

An important industrial mineral made of calcium and fluorine.

WHY ARE AMETHYSTS PURPLE?

They get their color from the traces of iron they contain.

Quartz crystals

WHAT CONTINENT HAS THE LARGEST RESERVES OF DIAMONDS?

Africa.

WHAT ARE THE MOST-MINED MINERALS?

Coal, bauxite, and iron.

WHO STUDIES ROCKS AND MINERALS?

Geologists.

WHAT ARE FOSSILS?

The remains of plants and animals—bones, shells, eggs, seeds—preserved for many thousands, and even millions, of years are called fossils. A body fossil is formed of actual parts of the organism. Other impressions, such as footprints and scratch marks, are known as trace fossils. Fossils are most often found in soft sedimentary rocks such as limestone and sandstone.

Pterodactyl fossil

Rapid-FIRE?

Nodosaur mummy

HAS FLESH EVER BEEN PRESERVED AS A FOSSIL?

Yes. Freeze-dried fossils found in Siberia still have flesh, even fur, on them. The bones, skin, and armor of this nodosaur found offshore in Alberta, Canada, are beautifully preserved.

WHAT ARE AMMONITES?

A group of extinct marine mollusks that lived at the same time as dinosaurs.

Ammonite fossil

WHAT IS AN EXPERT ON FOSSILS CALLED?

A paleontologist.

WHERE DOES THE WORD "FOSSIL" COME FROM?

It is rooted in the Latin word *fossilis*, meaning "dug up."

Uncovering a fossil

WHO DISCOVERED DINOSAURS?

Around 1819, scientists identified some fossils as belonging to "giants" they named *Megalosaurus*. In 1842 British scientist Richard Owen studied these fossils and noticed similarities among them and that they looked reptilian. He also realized that they were very different from any animals that now roamed Earth. Owen coined the name "dinosaurs," meaning "terrible lizards."

Richard Owen

HOW DO WE KNOW THE AGE OF A FOSSIL?

The age of a fossil is gauged by what is called radiometric, carbon-14 dating, which measures changes in its atomic structure. But carbon-14 cannot date fossils older than 50,000 years, such as those of dinosaurs. To date such fossils, other types of radiometric dating are used that calculate the age of the rocks above and below the sedimentary rock in which such a fossil was found.

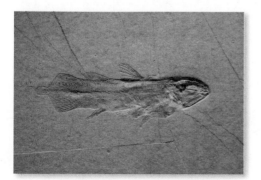

Ancient fish fossil on sandstone

WHY IS THE STUDY OF FOSSILS USEFUL?

Fossils, both plant and animal, are a valuable source of information on how life has evolved on Earth—they are a window into the past. They also provide insight on ecological, climatic, and environmental changes that have taken place over the ages.

Insect fossil in amber

Big?
HOW ARE FOSSILS FORMED?

The dinosaur dies in a river.

The body is covered with sediment. The flesh decomposes. The dinosaur becomes a fossil.

The sediments become rock. The skeleton is pressed.

The Earth's movements raise the layers of the rocks to the surface.

The rock erodes, exposing the fossil.

Fossil formation

When a plant or animal is buried quickly, it gets enclosed in sediment before it decomposes. As pressure transforms this sediment into rock, a hollow mold of the organism is formed. Gradually, minerals seep into this hollow and harden over time to form a detailed, three-dimensional cast. Soft tissue organisms are preserved as impressions between layers of sediment. Perfectly preserved fossils of insects and other small forms of life have also been found trapped inside hardened tree sap.

WHAT IS CONTINENTAL DRIFT?

In the early 20th century, German scientist Alfred Wegener termed the gradual movement of Earth's major landmasses—Europe, the Americas, Africa, Australia, Asia, and Antarctica—as "continental drift." The modern-day term, however, is plate tectonics. Wegener suggested that over geological time, landmasses may have pulled apart or pushed together to create new landforms. He found evidence for this when he discovered fossils in Norway that seemed to originate in a tropical climate.

Alfred Wegener

Rapid-FIRE?

FROM WHERE IN THE SUPERCONTINENT DID ANTARCTICA BREAK AWAY?

It was positioned between Australia and Africa.

Antarctica as part of the supercontinent

WHICH FOSSIL CONNECTS ALL THE SOUTHERN CONTINENTS?

Fossil remains of the fern *Glossopteris* are found in Australia, Antarctica, India, Africa, and South America.

WHICH CONTINENTS COLLIDED TO FORM THE ALPS?

Europe and Africa.

WHAT IS THE SAN ANDREAS FAULT IN CALIFORNIA, USA?

A fracture between two of Earth's tectonic plates.

San Andreas Fault, USA

WHY DO THE CONTINENTS MOVE?

The surface of Earth is broken into giant fragments called tectonic plates. The continents are situated on top of these tectonic plates, which carry them much like cargo on rafts. The plates move at rates of around 1 to 2 inches per year, and over millions of years this moves the continents over many thousands of miles.

Mountain ranges thrown upward by the collision of tectonic plates

HOW DO WE MEASURE PLATE TECTONICS?

Satellite tracking stations were initially used to measure plate tectonics. Currently, an accurate measurement can be made using GPS trackers. Radio telescopes also give an accurate reading.

Satellite tracking systems

Big ? WAS THERE EVER A SUPERCONTINENT?

Pangea
200 million years ago

Pangea

North America · Eurasia · South America · Africa · Antarctica · Australia

Laurasia & Gondwana
120 million years ago

Laurasia

Gondwana

North America · Eurasia · South America · Africa · Antarctica · Australia

A single landmass

In 1912, Alfred Wegener suggested that about 240 million years ago, Earth's surface comprised one supercontinent, Pangea, and the giant ocean Panthalassa. Pangaea started breaking up about 200 million years ago, and the pieces moved apart to form the continents as we recognize them today. In 1937, South African geologist Alexander du Toit modified this theory, suggesting that there were two original continents—Laurasia in the north and Gondwana to the south.

HOW WAS ANTARCTICA FORMED?

About 252 to 66 million years ago, Antarctica was lush with flora and fauna. The land broke away from other continents between 49 million to 17 million years ago, drifted toward the South Pole and froze. The ice sheet has an average thickness of 1.34 miles, which makes Antarctica the world's highest continent.

WHAT DO THE WORDS "STALACTITE" AND "STALAGMITE" MEAN?

Both "stalactite" and "stalagmite" originate from the Greek word *stalassein* meaning "to drip." The first use of both words goes back to the 17th century. Both stalactites and stalagmites are also called dripstones since they form from minerals in dripping water.

Stalactites and stalagmites can create some interesting shapes.

Rapid-FIRE?

WHAT IS THE EXPLORATION OF CAVES CALLED?

Caving, potholing, or spelunking.

Exploring a cave

WHAT IS THE STUDY OF CAVES CALLED?

Speleology.

Studying caves

IS IT TRUE THAT STALACTITES AND STALAGMITES GLOW IN THE DARK?

Yes. Limestone glows when exposed to intense light.

CAN STALACTITES APPEAR UNDERWATER?

Yes, stalactites, also called "hanging speleothems," have been found underwater, for example the Hells Bells in Mexico. They are hollow structures that expand conically downward. In addition to the carbonate that builds stalactites and stalagmites, bacteria and algae help in the formation of these underwater stalactites.

Hells Bells speleothems

HOW OLD ARE THE OLDEST STALACTITES AND STALAGMITES?

Limestone stalactites and stalagmites are formed extremely slowly: possibly only about 4 inches over a thousand years. Scientific studies have shown some to be very old, forming for as long as 190,000 years!

These formations could be thousands of years old.

WHICH IS THE LONGEST STALACTITE IN THE WORLD?

The 27-ft-long limestone stalactite thought to be the longest in the world is in Jeita Grotto, a limestone cave complex, 11 miles north of Beirut, the capital of Lebanon. It was discovered in 1836.

Jeita Grotto, Lebanon

Stalactites being formed

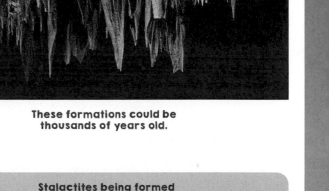

WHAT IS SPECIAL ABOUT THE DOOLIN CAVE OF IRELAND?

Poll-an-Ionain, a limestone cave in Doolin, Ireland, has the longest known free-hanging stalactite in Europe. It is 24 ft in length and is known as the Great Stalactite. The cave was discovered in 1952 and it is assumed that the Great Stalactite was formed over thousands and thousands of years. The Doolin Cave opened to the public in 2006.

The Great Stalactite, Doolin Cave, Ireland

Big ? ARE STALACTITES AND STALAGMITES ALWAYS FOUND IN PAIRS?

No, stalactites and stalagmites can occur singly. It is true, however, that stalagmites are usually formed on the ground from the same drip source that creates a stalactite on the ceiling of the cave. The simplest stalactite takes the form of a thin straw. As more and more of the mineral calcite is deposited, the downward growth takes the form of a cone. The calcite drip that reaches the ground forms a stalagmite, a bit like a spike with a rounded tip. It is possible that, over time, the stalagmite and stalactite may meet to form a column that extends from floor to ceiling.

WHAT ARE EARTHQUAKES?

The shuddering of the ground is called an earthquake. Some quakes are slight and barely noticeable, but others can be terrifying. The most violent ones occur around the edges of the plates that make up Earth's outer layers. Powerful earthquakes can bring down buildings and bridges, cause landslides, and sometimes destroy entire towns.

Fault

Epicenter

Upthrown block

Focus

Fault

How earthquakes happen

Downthrown block

Wave fronts

Rapid-FIRE ?

WHICH JAPANESE CITY DID AN EARTHQUAKE DEVASTATE IN 1995?

Kobe, in the Hyogo Prefecture.

Earthquake Memorial Park, Kobe, Japan

WHAT IS THE SAN ANDREAS FAULT?

The San Andreas Fault in California, USA, is where two of Earth's great plates slide past each other, often setting off earthquakes such as the one that destroyed San Francisco in 1906.

HOW LONG WAS THE LONGEST EARTHQUAKE?

The longest recorded earthquake happened near the coast of Sumatra, Indonesia, in 2004. It lasted almost 10 minutes—most earthquakes last less than a minute!

WHAT IS A TSUNAMI?

Earthquakes on the ocean floor trigger giant water waves called tsunamis. Tsunamis travel through the water at up to 500 miles per hour. As they approach the land, the water piles up into deadly waves many feet high, causing massive destruction as they hit the coast.

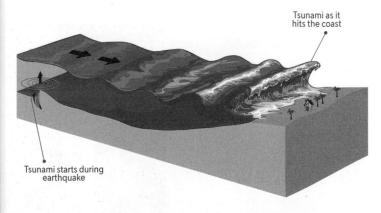

Tsunami as it hits the coast

Tsunami starts during earthquake

How underwater earthquakes set off tsunamis

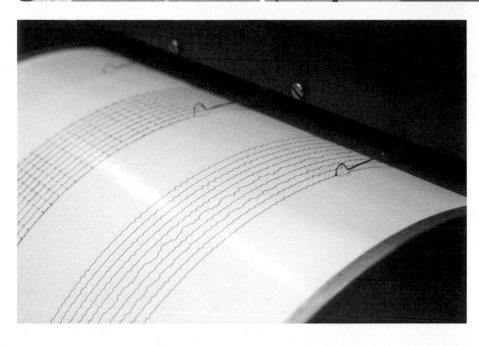

HOW IS AN EARTHQUAKE MEASURED?

A machine called a seismometer detects ground tremors and records them on a seismograph. The size of the earthquake is assessed on the Richter scale, which goes from one (slight tremor) to over nine (severe earthquake).

Measuring the intensity of an earthquake

WHAT ARE EARTHQUAKE ZONES?

These are areas that are particularly prone to earthquakes. Most of these fall on or near the edges of the tectonic plates. Many major cities such as Los Angeles, Mexico City, and Tokyo are in earthquake zones.

Devastation caused by an earthquake, Japan

Earth's tectonic plates

North American plate

North American plate

Juan de Fuca plate

Eurasian plate

Caribbean plate

Cocos plate

Arabian plate

Indian plate

Philippine plate

Pacific plate

Pacific plate

African plate

Nazca plate

South American plate

Australian plate

Big? WHAT CAUSES AN EARTHQUAKE?

The huge tectonic plates that make up Earth's surface usually glide past each other. But at times they clash and get jammed. When this happens, the rock bends and stretches until the pressure of currents under the plates causes them to jerk apart, sending shock waves in all directions. The point where an earthquake begins underground is the hypocenter, or focus. The point on the surface above is the epicenter and this is where the earth quakes most violently.

HOW DOES A QUAKE SPREAD OUT?

There are two main kinds of earthquake waves. Body waves remain underground and can travel at huge speeds, vibrating all around the world. Surface waves travel out along the surface from the epicenter. They are much slower, but they do the real damage. Surface waves are of two kinds: Love waves shake the ground from side to side, while Rayleigh waves shake the ground up and down and seem to roll through sandy or muddy ground like waves in the ocean.

WHAT ARE VOLCANOES?

Volcanoes are places where molten rock, called magma, from Earth's core comes up through the ground. Sometimes, it just oozes slowly onto the surface as a red-hot stream called lava. At other times, the magma builds up underground until the pressure finally causes it to explode out of the Earth as an eruption.

Rapid-FIRE?

WHERE WAS **POMPEII**?

Discovered in the 18th century, Pompeii was a Roman town in Italy that was buried almost instantly when Mount Vesuvius, in Italy, erupted in 79 CE. The remains found under the ash of the eruption are almost perfectly preserved.

The ruins of Pompeii

WHAT WAS THE **DEADLIEST ERUPTION EVER IN THE USA**?

Mount St. Helens, in Washington State, erupted in 1980, entirely blowing away the top and side of the mountain, flattening an area of over 300 square miles!

Mount St. Helens, USA

IS THERE AN **ACTIVE VOLCANO IN INDONESIA**?

Mount Semeru, on the island of Java, has been active since 1967.

DO **VOLCANOES DO ANY GOOD**?

Volcanic eruptions cause tremendous damage, but soil formed from volcanic ash is extremely fertile. Volcanic rocks are also used in building and chemical industries. In Iceland, which has 35 active volcanoes, their heat is used to provide the country with plentiful energy, known as geothermal power.

CAN WATER BURST OUT OF THE GROUND LIKE LAVA?

It can, in the form of a hot spring, where underground water, heated by magma inside Earth, bubbles up through the surface. This hot, underground water can also burst out in a ferocious jet of steam and hot water called a geyser, which can shoot up hundreds of feet high.

Hot springs

WHAT ARE HOT SPOTS?

These are areas of great heat in Earth's mantle, where plumes of hot magma rise under the crust. Hot spots have high volcanic activity. Hawaii in the Pacific Ocean is located over a hot spot.

A volcanic eruption

Earth's magma oozing to the surface

ARE THERE VOLCANOES THAT DON'T ERUPT?

Some active volcanoes erupt with great regularity, but others are quiet for periods and erupt only now and then. When they are not erupting, volcanoes are said to be dormant, or sleeping. If they have never erupted in recorded history, they are considered extinct. Edinburgh Castle is built on an extinct volcano.

Edinburgh Castle, Scotland

Big? ARE ALL VOLCANOES THE SAME?

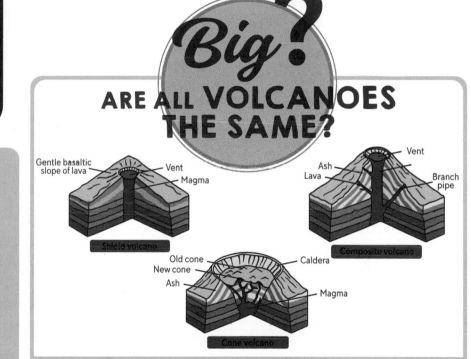

Types of volcanoes

No, there are three main kinds of volcanoes: shield, cone, and composite. Magma that is low in silica is very fluid. It gushes out from cracks in the ground and flows out over wide areas, hardening to form what are called shield volcanoes. When magma contains a lot of silica, it does not flow as easily and piles up around the vent (the place where it comes out of the ground). Successive eruptions build up a "typical" volcano shape, like Mount Fuji in Japan and Mount Kilimanjaro in Kenya. Composite volcanoes are built up from alternate layers of lava and ash. During each eruption, the ash falls slowly to settle on top of the lava flow.

WHAT IS WEATHERING?

It is a process in which hard rock and minerals on the surface of Earth gradually break down and change form because they are exposed to wind, water, salt, and varying temperatures. Weathering is the first step in the formation of soil. There are two types of weathering: mechanical and chemical. In the first type, rocks break up into smaller fragments, while in the second, the original material transforms into another substance.

Weathering and erosion can shape very strange landscape features

Rapid-Fire ?

WHAT IS SCREE?

Loose rocks of roughly the same size littered on steep mountain slopes.

Scree at the base of a mountain slope

DO RABBITS HELP EROSION BY THEIR BURROWING?

Yes, and also by grazing grass down to very low levels.

A rabbit burrow

HOW QUICKLY DOES LAND GET WORN AWAY?

At a rate of approximately 1.3 inches over 100 years.

WHAT KIND OF CONDITIONS SPEED UP WEATHERING?

The presence of water and changing temperature. Weathering happens less in very hot and dry areas, as well as places that are extremely cold and dry, where the temperature does not change much.

HOW DOES WATER WEATHER ROCKS?

Flowing river water dislodges and drags stones and rocks lying or embedded in the riverbed. These rocks hit other rocks and a process of disintegration begins. Water also dissolves rock salts, turning the minerals in the rock into a clay called kaolin. The salty water of coastlines can seep into rock pores and eventually evaporate, leaving behind salt crystals.

Low water levels clearly show the erosion of the riverbank

WHAT IS GROUNDWATER?

Rainwater seeps below the surface of the Earth and soaks the soil. When there is more water than the soil can absorb, it can seep even farther down until it is surrounded by rocks, creating a kind of storage area, known as an aquifer. The water here is groundwater, and the upper level of water is called the water table.

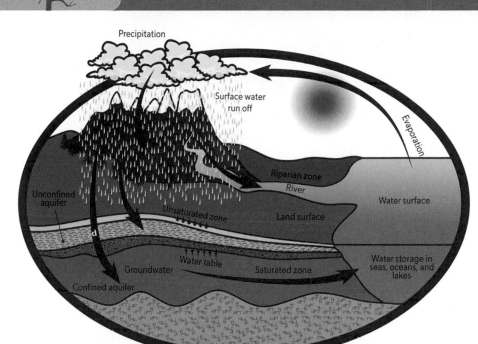

Formation of underground aquifers

Big WHAT IS THE DIFFERENCE BETWEEN WEATHERING AND EROSION?

Water erosion

Weathering is the result of rocks wearing down because of the actions of the forces of nature. It is a natural process. During weathering, the rocks in their changed form remain in the same place—there is no movement of material. Erosion, on the other hand, happens when the broken-down rocks are carried away by water, ice, wind, or gravity, and the remains are deposited far away from the place where the change initially happened.

HOW ARE WEATHERING AND EROSION MEASURED?

Some abrupt and high-impact erosion and weathering is obvious to the eyes, but much of the weathering on a rock surface is difficult to assess unless it is mapped over a long period of time. Changes in the roughness of rock are measured using scientific methods, which involve collecting samples.

Geologists taking rock samples

WHAT IS HONEYCOMB WEATHERING?

When salt water collects on the rough surface of rocks, or seeps into cracks, it evaporates, leaving behind salt crystals. Over time, these crystals alter the rock, forming hundreds and thousands of tightly joined pits called honeycombs that are a classic example of both physical and chemical weathering.

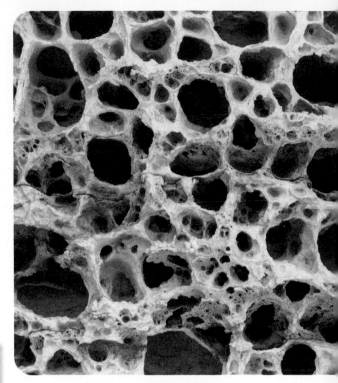

Rock honeycombed by chemical and physical weathering

WHY DOES A SMALL ROCK WEATHER FASTER THAN A LARGE ONE?

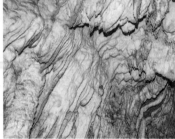

A frill-like pattern on stone created by weathering over time

Weathering affects the surface of rocks and minerals. The greater the exposed surface area of a rock, the faster it weathers. A smaller rock usually exposes more of its surface as compared to a large rock and, therefore, weathers much faster.

CAN TREES CAUSE WEATHERING?

Yes, trees can break up large rocks. Seeds may be deposited in the cracks and spaces of rock clusters and germinate there. As the plant grows, the roots crack the rock further, and may even break it into many pieces.

Big? WHAT IS THE DIFFERENCE BETWEEN PHYSICAL AND CHEMICAL WEATHERING?

An arch formed by the gradual physical weathering of rock

Physical weathering is also known as mechanical weathering. It is a process, initiated by humans, plants, or animals, which breaks down rocks and minerals on the surface of Earth. It changes just the shape or size of the rocks and minerals. Chemical weathering, on the other hand, happens when the chemical composition of the rock and soil changes, forming new chemical combinations and a different internal structure.

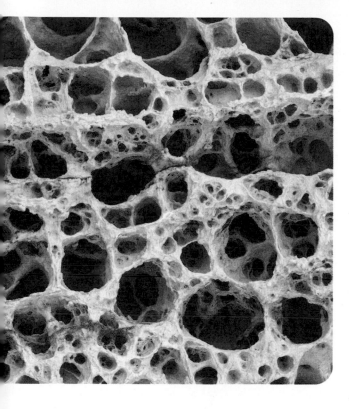

WHAT IS **CARBONATION?**

Decaying leaves and plant matter emit carbon dioxide, which is also present in the air around us. Carbon dioxide dissolves in water to create carbonic acid through a process called carbonation.

This acid can, over time, dissolve rocks, especially limestone. Limestone is a soft rock that consists mainly of calcium carbonate, which reacts with rainwater, dissolving away to create huge caves and cave complexes.

Soil and rock washed away over time to leave an underground cavity

HOW DOES **FROST BREAK UP ROCKS?**

When water collects in the cracks of a rock, it can freeze when temperatures drop. The ice expands and the pressure can split the rock. In cold, mountain regions, one can even hear gunshotlike cracks as rocks are split apart by frost.

Frost can crack and split even large rocks.

Rapid-Fire ?

Haloclasty

WHAT IS **WEATHERING CAUSED BY SALT CRYSTALS CALLED?**

Haloclasty.

Fairy inkcap fungi

DO **BACTERIA AND FUNGI SPEED UP WEATHERING?**

Yes. They weaken the rock by taking out chemicals like silica and phosphorus for their nutrition.

Lichen on stone

WHAT IS **BIOLOGICAL WEATHERING?**

When lichen and moss growing on a rock create an environment that causes rocks to break down both physically and chemically.

WHAT IS **WIND?**

Wind is moving air, ranging from a light, gentle breeze to a very strong and fast-moving storm capable of great destruction. Air moves because the Sun warms some places more than the others, creating differences in air pressure, which causes the air to be pushed around in the form of air currents.

Seeing the wind in motion

From space, the "eye" of the hurricane is clearly visible

Big? WHAT ARE **HURRICANES?**

A hurricane is a giant, spiraling tropical storm that can reach wind speeds of over 159 miles per hour and unleash more than 264 billion gallons of rain! It begins as thunderstorms that are set off by moist air rising over the warm ocean. If the water is warm enough, the thunderstorms join together, growing bigger as they begin to spiral across the ocean. As the hurricane grows, it spins faster and tighter around its center, or "eye," which remains a very calm area of low pressure. A hurricane can be as much as 500 miles across and can take 18 hours to pass over. In the South Pacific and Indian Ocean hurricanes are known as cyclones, and in the Northwest Pacific Ocean, as typhoons.

WHAT IS **LA NIÑA?**

Meaning "the little girl" in Spanish, La Niña is a climatic pattern caused by a buildup of cooler-than-normal waters in the tropical Pacific, the area of the Pacific Ocean between the Tropic of Cancer and the Tropic of Capricorn. The drastic drop in ocean-surface temperature affects patterns of rainfall, atmospheric pressure, and atmospheric circulation around the world.

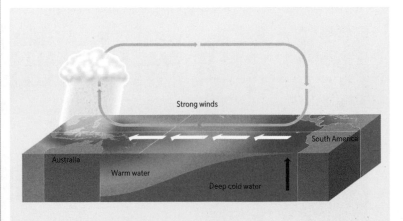

Strong winds

South America

Australia

Warm water

Deep cold water

Climatic patterns caused by La Niña

Rapid-Fire?

WHEN WAS THE **DEADLIEST HURRICANE** EVER RECORDED?

More than 20,000 people died in the Caribbean during the Great Hurricane of 1780, when winds may have reached a phenomenal 200 miles per hour.

WHAT IS THE **BEST DEFENSE AGAINST A HURRICANE?**

An accurate forecast of its path in order to inform people to get out of its way.

Blizzard

WHAT IS A **BLIZZARD?**

A prolonged winter storm that combines heavy snowfall, strong winds of more than 35 miles per hour, and very low temperature, all resulting in poor visibility.

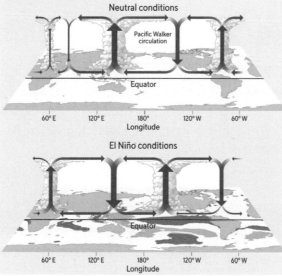

How El Niño heats up the atmosphere

WHAT IS **EL NIÑO?**

El Niño, or "the little boy" in Spanish, is a climatic pattern that describes the unusual warming of surface waters in the eastern equatorial Pacific Ocean. El Niño often produces some of the hottest years on record because of the huge amount of heat that rises from Pacific waters into the atmosphere.

WHAT ARE **TORNADOES?**

A tornado, also called a twister, is a violently rotating funnel of air, set off by giant thunderclouds called supercells. The vortex, known as a landspout, is a whirling mass of air hanging from the base of the cloud down to the ground, like the hose of a vacuum cleaner. Over water, a tornado forms a waterspout. Tornadoes can also occur as two or more spinning vortexes spinning around each other.

A tornado reaching down from the clouds

WHAT ARE SANDSTORMS?

When strong winds storm across sandy deserts, they lift huge amounts of sand into the air and forcefully blow it around in what is called a sandstorm. The force and speed of the wind can carry the sand for thousands of miles before depositing it again. The coarseness of the particles can make a sandstorm really devastating. Smaller grains can remain suspended in the air for a long time.

Sand blowing across a desert

A mushroom rock

WHAT IS A MUSHROOM ROCK?

A rock that is shaped like a mushroom! What's interesting is how the rock gets that shape. The strong winds blowing across desert landscapes erode the base of enormous boulders more than the top. Over many years, this results in a thin stem supporting a broad cap—a mushroom rock.

Quick-FIRE ?

HOW OLD IS THE KALAHARI DESERT?

About 60 million years old!

WHAT DESERT WERE DINOSAUR EGGS DISCOVERED IN?

The Gobi Desert.

Dinosaur egg fossil

Stargazing in the Atacama

IN A YEAR, HOW MANY CLOUD-FREE NIGHTS DOES THE ATACAMA DESERT GET?

330 cloud-free nights, which makes it a great place for astronomical observations.

WHAT IS AN **ERG?**

A large area full of sand dunes in a sandy desert is called an erg. Because they are formed by the wind, it is likely that their shape, or their number, may change over a period of time. A large erg can spread over many miles.

Erg Chebbi, Merzouga, Morocco

WHAT ARE **BARCHANS?**

When there is a lot of loose sand in a desert and the wind blows constantly in one direction, it builds up crescent-shaped sand dunes, whose tips point against the wind. Large barchans can be very wide and very high.

A Barchan

Big **?**

HOW DO **SANDSTORMS IMPACT LANDSCAPES?**

Sand dunes in the eastern Sahara

Not only can sandstorms damage and bury plants and seedlings, when sand is carried in the wind, the suspended particles trap the Sun's heat before it can reach the ground. As a result, the air in the area where this sand is deposited or remains suspended becomes warmer and drier. It cannot retain moisture anymore. The increase in temperature and decreased precipitation reduce plant growth and result in greater soil erosion, which leads to changes in the landscape.

WHAT IS THE **ENCHANTED MESA?**

A butte is an isolated hill with steep sides and a flat top created by the gradual erosion of the earth around it by water, wind, or ice. The Enchanted Mesa is a sandstone butte in New Mexico where the Acoma tribe lived until a heavy storm and a landslide destroyed the only access to the peak, forcing them to move elsewhere.

Enchanted Mesa, New Mexico, USA

WHAT IS AN ICE AGE?

A very long period of time, it could be millions of years, during which major parts of Earth are covered with ice because of a significant drop in temperature. Geologists say that the most recent was the Little Ice Age, which started in the 16th century in Europe and many regions across the world. and reached its peak in 1850.

Quick-FIRE?

DOES ANTARCTICA HOLD MOST OF THE WORLD'S FRESH WATER?

Yes, almost 80 percent of all the fresh water on Earth.

Fresh water locked as Ice

HOW OLD IS GLACIER ICE?

In Antarctica some ice is over one million years old.

IS ANTARCTICA A DESERT?

It is a polar desert, since there is very little precipitation.

HOW MUCH OF THE WORLD IS COVERED BY ICE?

Almost 10 percent of Earth's total landmass is covered by ice. This includes glaciers, ice caps, and ice sheets. Glaciers cover 9 million square miles. During the last ice age, 32 percent of the total land area was covered by ice.

Ice cap over Greenland

DO ICE AGES CHANGE LANDSCAPES?

Yes, ice ages create significant changes in landscapes. From when it was covered in ice to the later warming up of Earth, ice ages have resulted in the formation of lakes, rivers, valleys, and fjords. Both Northern Europe and America have seen numerous changes in landforms due to ice ages.

WHAT ARE THE LARGEST BODIES OF ICE IN THE WORLD?

In today's world, the ice sheets of Antarctica and Greenland. An ice sheet is a continuous mass of ice covering more than 31,000 square miles. The ice sheet in Antarctica covers 8.5 million sq miles. It is between 1 to 4 miles thick and holds 18.6 million square miles of ice. The Greenland ice sheet covers about 1 million square miles.

Antarctica

A frozen landscape

Perito Moreno Glacier, Argentina

WHAT CAUSES THE END OF AN ICE AGE?

The rotation and revolution of Earth, the amount of solar radiation, and the amount of carbon dioxide in the atmosphere are all factors that contribute to a warming up of Earth, which ends an ice age. Changes in ocean currents also have a major effect on temperatures on Earth.

Big? HAVE THERE BEEN MANY ICE AGES?

There have been at least five major ice ages in Earth's history: the Huronian, Cryogenian, Andean-Saharan, late Paleozoic, and Quaternary. The study of rocks dates the Huronian around 2.1 billion years ago. The Cryogenic, around 700 million years ago, may have caused Earth to be almost totally frozen, like a snowball. The Andean-Saharan Ice Age happened around 400 million years ago. The late Paleozoic, around 360 million years ago, had extensive polar ice caps. The Quaternary Age began around 2.5 million years ago. Currently, Earth is in an interglacial period—it is between ice ages.

Melting glaciers and icebergs

HOW DO WE KNOW THAT ICE ONCE COVERED AN AREA?

A study of rocks found in an area reveals much about its past. Debris and sediments left behind by ice can provide evidence of an area's history. Also, land eroded by ice shows certain typical landforms such as glaciated valleys with cirques, arêtes, and horns. All these indicate the presence of ice some time in the past.

An esker

WHAT IS AN ESKER?

Sometimes a stream cuts a channel under a slow-moving glacier, creating a long, winding ridge of sand and gravel that is called an esker. Before the glacier melted, the banks of these streams were defined by glacier ice. The deposited gravel now stands high above the surrounding land.

Elephant Foot Glacier, Greenland

Big? WHAT ARE CIRQUES, ARÊTES, AND HORNS?

A cirque

Cirques are formed when a glacier wears away a mountainside leaving a rounded hollow with steep, almost vertical, walls. Such basins are usually found at the top of a glacial valley. Arêtes are knife-edged ridges between cirques that are created when glacial erosion occurs on both sides of a mountain. Horns are peaks created when three or more cirques are formed back to back.

WHAT ARE **DRUMLINS?**

Rounded or mound-shaped hills created by glacial ice, drumlins are often found in clusters. They are largely made up of sediment deposited by a glacier and can vary greatly in size. The name derives from a Gaelic word *droimin* meaning "smallest ridges."

*Rapid-*FIRE **?**

WHAT IS A KETTLE?

A small pit left behind by a glacier that now forms a pond.

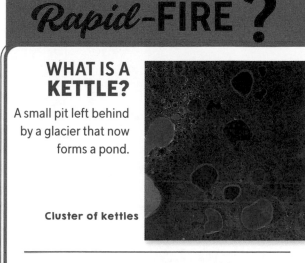

Cluster of kettles

WHAT IS A **KAME?**

A small hill formed by deposits left by a melting glacier.

Kame

WHERE IS THE **ESKERS PROVINCIAL PARK LOCATED?**

British Columbia, Canada.

WHAT IS A **GLACIAL ERRATIC?**

A rock resting on rocks from which it differs drastically is a glacial erratic. It would have been transported to a location many miles away from its place of origin by glacial erosion. An erratic can vary in size from a small rock to a very big boulder. Studying such rocks helps scientists define the path of glacial movement.

Glacial erractic

WHAT ARE **MORAINE RIDGES?**

The variety of loose rocks and sediments dumped over a landscape give evidence about the type of glacier and glaciation that took place in the area. A moraine ridge is the landform created by the debris left by a glacier after it has moved away. Moraine ridges are given names according to the size of debris and how they were formed. Examples are: lateral moraine, recessional moraine, medial moraine, and ground moraine.

Moraine ridge

HAVE PEOPLE CHANGED THE EARTH?

Since the time humans first started making permanent homes, they have harnessed nature to meet their various needs. Landscapes have been transformed—whether by cutting trees, clearing jungles, fishing, raising animals, growing crops, constructing houses, or setting up industry. The increase in human population and many other changes linked to human lifestyle, need, and development have altered the face of Earth to a very large extent.

Are humans greening Earth or turning it brown?

Rapid-FIRE ?

IS CORAL UNDER THREAT DUE TO GLOBAL WARMING?

Yes, because coral is very sensitive to temperature change.

Coral

HOW MUCH FOREST ARE WE LOSING EVERY YEAR TO DEFORESTATION?

Too much! Approximately 100,000 sq miles a year.

Cutting down forests for wood

WHAT IS SMOG?

Smoke added to fog creates smog.

CAN GLOBAL WARMING AFFECT ISLAND NATIONS?

The melting of glaciers as a result of global warming is likely to raise sea levels. This will most seriously affect islands. It is possible that many countries, such as the Maldives and Kiribati, could completely vanish under the ocean.

WHAT IS DESERTIFICATION?

Trees and plants hold onto the soil, enrich it, and help balance moisture in the surrounding areas. When trees are cut down and grasslands are destroyed, the once-fertile land is exposed to the elements and slowly becomes dry and dusty. This is called desertification.

Soil exposed to the elements

WHAT IS **AIR POLLUTION?**

When waste gases from industries are released into the atmosphere in large quantities, they add poisonous fumes to the air. This is known as pollution. Cars also release gases as they burn gasoline and diesel, harming air quality and adding to air pollution.

Air pollution

WHAT IS **DEFORESTATION?**

Trees take a long time to grow. Deforestation is the removal of trees, especially when they are cut down in large numbers without new ones being planted. It turns a thick forest of large trees into barren land.

Tree stumps in a cleared forest area

WHAT IS **RIVER POLLUTION?**

When untreated human and industrial waste is drained into a river, it fills the water with toxic materials and sediments. This pollution can destroy the ecosystem of the river and make the water unfit, even dangerous, to use.

Plastic waste along a riverbank

Big? WHAT ARE **GLOBAL WARMING AND CLIMATE CHANGE?**

A drought-affected landscape

Global warming is the rising of average temperatures across Earth—of the land, the oceans, or atmosphere. Human activities, such as setting up large-scale industries have had a significant impact over time. They release enormous quantities of greenhouse gases, which trap heat in Earth's atmosphere, warming the planet. Climate change describes the extremes in weather that bring sudden and long periods of drought, flood, bitter cold, and other conditions. that are not typical to the climate of a region. These are all related to the disruption caused by global warming and the long-term impact of human beings and their lifestyles on the environment.

WHAT IS A COAST?

Land that runs along a sea or ocean is called a coast. The edge of the land where it meets the water is called the coastline. Coasts can be wide swathes of soft, sandy beaches, narrow, rocky stretches, or sheer cliff faces. Coastlines are given their shape by waves, currents, and tides. They are ever changing and form an important and unique environment.

Stretch of the Californian coast

HOW IS A ROCK ARCH CREATED?

When a high, rocky outcrop juts out into the water, the crashing of waves over the years erodes the base. If the layer of rock higher up stays intact as the base is worn through, a natural rock arch is carved out.

Rock arch along the coast of Lake Michigan, USA

Beach at Eype, UK

WHAT IS A SHINGLE BEACH?

When stone, pebbles, and small rocks are deposited along the coast, they create a porous layer that is not as tightly packed together as sand is. These are shingle beaches. Common to New Zealand, Japan, and the United Kingdom, shingle beaches support little vegetation and mostly have lichen-covered rocks.

HOW ARE WAVES FORMED?

When sunlight enters Earth's atmosphere, the energy from the Sun heats up the air. This hot air expands and rises, creating space under it for cooler air to rush in. This movement causes winds. Winds that blow over the surface of ocean water transfer energy to the water, setting off ripples. As these ripples get bigger, they become waves.

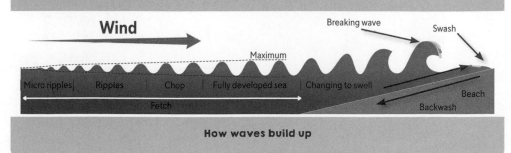

Wind

Breaking wave

Swash

Maximum

Micro ripples | Ripples | Chop | Fully developed sea | Changing to swell

Beach

Fetch

Backwash

How waves build up

*Rapid-*FIRE**?**

WHICH IS THE LONGEST NATURAL SAND BEACH?

Cox's Bazar in Bangladesh.

Cox's Bazar, Bangladesh

WHAT IS AN ARCHIPELAGO?

A group, or a chain, of many islands.

Lofoten Archipelago, Norway

WHICH IS THE **LONGEST BEACH?**

Praia do Cassino in Brazil stretches for 149 miles.

Praia do Cassino, Brazil

WHICH COUNTRY HAS THE LONGEST COASTLINE?

Canada. The coastline measures 125,500 miles.

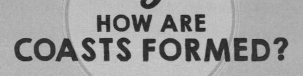

Waves shape coastlines

*Big***?**
HOW ARE COASTS FORMED?

When waves, tidal waves in particular, hit land, the force of water has the power to break and crush rocks and to erode the soil. But they also bring in seashells, seaweed, other organic matter and debris from the ocean, which all gets mixed and deposited among the crushed rocks to shape the coastline. Coasts are formed over hundreds of years and can be quite changeable with time as tidal waves constantly crush, erode, wash away, bring in, and deposit materials.

ARE **WAVES TRAVELING BODIES OF WATER?**

No. The water itself does not travel but only moves up and down—it is energy from wind that is transferred in the form of a wave. The energy is transferred through the water in a circular motion. While waves move like a relay team transferring energy, the water goes around like a roller on a conveyor belt.

DOES THE OCEAN WEAR AWAY LAND?

Ocean waves constantly crash into coasts, crushing rocks and pebbles. Rising waves hurl small rocks onto coastal cliffs, eroding them or tearing away at their base until they collapse. Waves and water currents carry sand and gravel that can alter coastlines. The ocean and its waves can certainly wear away the land.

Coastlines are constantly battered by waves.

WHAT IS A SEA STACK?

A sea stack is a vertical column of rock near a coast. This column is the remains of limestone cliffs that have been battered by the sea from both sides. At first, the waves carve out deep caves in the cliffs, which then gradually collapse, leaving behind the steep stack of rocks.

A sea stack

Rapid-FIRE ?

WHAT IS UNIQUE ABOUT TWELVE APOSTLES MARINE NATIONAL PARK, AUSTRALIA?

It has 12 sea rock stacks.

The Twelve Apostles

WHAT IS A TOMBOLO?

A landform that attaches an island to the mainland by a spit or sandbar.

Tombolo

WHICH IS THE LARGEST BLOWHOLE?

Kiama Blowhole in Australia.

WHAT ARE BEACH GROINS?

Man-made shore protection measures to reduce erosion. Constructed of wood or stone, groins control the movement of water rushing onto the beach and prevent sand from being swept away by the waves. A number of groins usually run perpendicular to the shore and extend up to the water.

Beach groins

WHAT IS A BAY BAR?

When the movement of waves deposits gravel and sand in a way that prevents access to a bay, it builds up a bay bar. The existence of the bar creates a shallow lake known as a lagoon that is separated from the ocean.

Bay bar

Big? WHAT IS A SPIT?

A spit

A spit is a narrow, extended piece of land that develops where a coastline sharply turns in toward the landmass. Attached to the coast at one end, the spit seems to grow out of it, as the movement of waves and tides deposits sand and pebbles at the angle of the landmass. The other end extends out into the ocean, growing longer over time as more debris accumulates along it.

Kiama Blowhole, Australia

WHAT IS A BLOWHOLE?

Sometimes, the rocks along a coastline have a crevice or hole just above the low-tide mark. When the high tide rushes in, the crevice fills up with water, which tries to escape through this narrow hole. The buildup of pressure sprays out the water as an upward plume with a loud sound. This is a blowhole. Over time, a blowhole can create caves or even a pool of water near the coast.

ARE OCEANS AND SEAS DIFFERENT?

The difference lies in their depth, area, and variety of marine life. An ocean is deeper and covers a greater area compared to the sea. On the other hand, a sea has more diverse plant and animal life. There are fewer plants in an ocean since there are large areas where sunlight does not penetrate. The deep-sea creatures found in the darkness of oceans are unique.

Life underwater

HOW OLD ARE OCEANS?

The oceans were formed between 4.2 and 3.8 billion years ago. After Earth cooled to below 212 °F, all the gaseous water in the atmosphere condensed and, over a period of time, filled the Earth's basin to form the oceans.

Big?
WHICH ARE THE MAJOR OCEANS?

An ocean is a huge, continuous body of salt water. Oceanographers identify five major oceans on the basis of geography and the continents that surround them. These are the Pacific, Atlantic, Indian, Arctic, and Southern (also known as Antarctic) Oceans. They cover about two-thirds of Earth's surface and contain about 97 percent of the world's water.

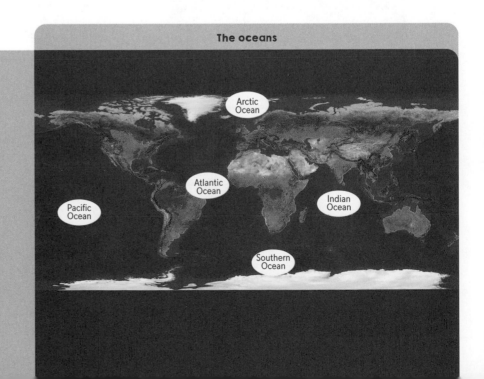
The oceans

The Pacific Ocean

WHICH IS THE BIGGEST OCEAN?

The Pacific is the biggest and deepest ocean. It covers a third of Earth's surface and has an area of 112 million miles^2, holding more than 435 million miles^3 of water. It is so big that all the continents could fit within its area.

Rapid-FIRE ?

WHAT IS THE AVERAGE DEPTH OF OCEANS?

About 8,950 ft.

Deep, dark depths

WHAT IS THE DEEPEST POINT ON EARTH'S SURFACE?

The Mariana Trench in the western Pacific is 36,300 ft deep.

Artist's impression of the Mariana Trench

WHAT IS THE TOTAL VOLUME OF WATER IN THE OCEANS?

An estimated 321 million miles^3 of water.

CAN THE DEEP OCEAN FLOOR BE MAPPED?

Ocean floors are mapped using sound equipment and robot submarines. Sonar systems send out high-frequency pulses. The time it takes for the sound pulse to echo back from the ocean floor gives an idea as to the depth of the ocean.

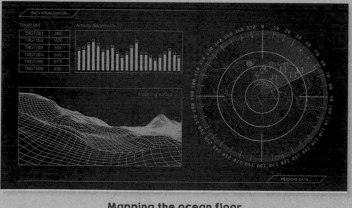

Mapping the ocean floor

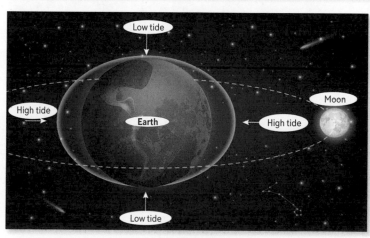

Low tide

High tide

Earth

Moon

High tide

Low tide

The Moon's influence

WHAT CAUSES TIDES?

Water level on the surface of the oceans rises and falls to create tides. Tides are a result of gravitational forces of the Moon and the Sun as well as the centrifugal forces of Earth's spin. The total amount of water does not change, it just rises at one place while receding at the other.

WHY IS IT COLDER IN THE MOUNTAINS?

As air expands, it becomes cooler. Air in the mountains, where the altitude (height above sea level) is higher, is under less pressure than air at lower altitudes because it is not being so compressed by the air above it. As a result, it expands and makes mountainous areas cold.

High mountain ranges

Rapid-FIRE ?

WHAT IS THE **WORLD'S HIGHEST MOUNTAIN?**

Mount Everest in the Himalayas in Asia, with its peak at 29,000 ft above sea level.

Mount Everest, China-Nepal border

WHAT IS **A SYNCLINE AND AN ANTICLINE?**

In rocks, the down-fold is a syncline and the up-fold is an anticline.

Syncline   Anticline

How rocks fold

WHAT IS **JAPAN'S HIGHEST MOUNTAIN?**

Japan's highest mountain, peaking at 12,388 ft, is Mount Fuji, an active volcano that sits on a triple junction of tectonic activity. Interestingly, it is made up of three different volcanoes. At the base is Komitake, in the middle, Kofuji, and at the top is Mount Fuji. The volcano last erupted in December, 1707.

Mount Fuji, Japan

Mont Blanc

NAME **EUROPE'S HIGHEST MOUNTAIN**

Mont Blanc in the Alps, on the French-Italian border.

Big? HOW ARE MOUNTAINS CREATED?

Mountain range

The collision of tectonic plates pushes up mountains.

Most of the world's greatest mountain ranges—the Himalayas, the Andes, the Rockies, the Caucasus, and the Alps—were created as Earth's tectonic plates collided. As the huge tectonic masses crashed into each other, they forced the layers of rock to fold. This is why these mountains form long, narrow ranges along the edges of continents. Mountains are also created as powerful earthquakes move Earth's crust and lift up huge blocks of rock. Volcanic eruptions can also create mountains.

Snow on the peaks and higher slopes never melts.

WHY ARE SOME MOUNTAINS SNOWCAPPED?

As altitude increases, the air gets colder. There comes a certain height, called the snow line, above which it is always too cold for the snow to melt, which is why some mountaintops are snowcapped all year round. The snow line is at 16,400 ft in the tropics, 8,858 ft in the Alps and at sea level at the poles.

DID MOUNTAINS ALWAYS EXIST?

It takes many millions of years to form mountains. Most of the world's highest mountains were formed quite recently in Earth's history, and are quite young in geological terms. The Himalayan mountain range was formed within the last 40 million years and is still growing.

WHERE DO RIVERS START AND END?

Rivers start off as small springs and streams high in the mountains. As they tumble downhill, they are joined by other streams, called tributaries, and become wider as they flow farther. Upon reaching flat plains, they flow smoothly and deeply until they empty their waters into the ocean or a lake.

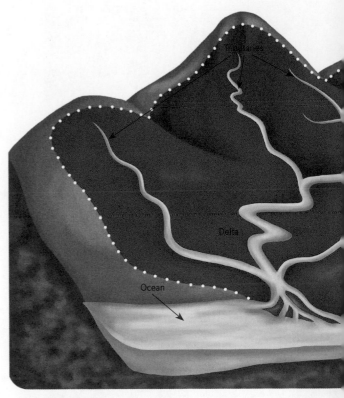

Tributaries

Delta

Ocean

The life of a river

WHAT IS A DELTA?

As a river reaches the ocean or a lake and slows down, sediment—sand, silt, and mud—builds up at its mouth, blocking its flow. The river then breaks up into several individual strands of water that make their way to the larger water body. The Nile forms a classic delta formation as the river enters into the Mediterranean Sea.

HOW DO RIVERS SHAPE THE LAND?

Over many thousands of years, rivers can wear away the land. First, they carve downward to create deep, V-shaped valleys. Then they swing sideways to widen these valleys, eventually creating broad plains that are frequently covered in fine silt.

Rapid-FIRE?

HOW LOUD IS THE ROAR OF ZIMBABWE'S VICTORIA FALLS?

With 368 inches^3 of water falling every second, the roar can be heard from 25 miles away!

Victoria Falls, Zimbabwe

WHAT IS THE WORLD'S LONGEST RIVER?

The Nile, in Egypt, flows over 4,146 miles.

The Nile River

WHAT IS THE HIGHEST WATERFALL?

Angel Falls in Venezuela, which plunge 3,211 ft vertically.

How a river collects water

Snow

Rainfall

Precipitation

Overland flows

Underground sources

Big ?
HOW DO RIVERS KEEP FLOWING?

Rivers are kept running by the addition of water from rainfall or melting snow. Even when it does not rain, underground reservoirs (water reserves) keep rivers flowing and supplied with water. When it rains, a lot of water seeps and sinks into the ground, to surface somewhere else as a spring. Over thousands of years, rivers can carve huge valleys out of solid rock with a wide floodplain (which is a flat area that catches the overflow when the river is full).

WHY DO RIVERS HAVE WINDING PATHS?

As rivers flow over more level, flat lands, they slow down and begin to deposit a lot of the rock, sand, and silt they carried down the mountains. The way the river builds up these deposits on one side and wears away the banks on others causes it to meander and wind its way across the plains.

Rivers slow down and meander across plains.

HOW DO WATERFALLS FORM?

A waterfall develops when the bed of the river changes from hard to soft rock. Since the force of the water wears away soft rock faster, the level of the softer riverbed drops, and the river plunges over a ledge of hard rock. The depth of the fall increases over time as more and more of the soft rock is washed away.

The sheer drop of Angel Falls, Venezuela

WHAT ARE GLACIERS?

The word "glacier" comes from the French word *glace*, meaning ice. A glacier is a huge, slow-moving mass of ice. Glaciers are generally seen in mountainous regions where temperatures always remain close to freezing and an enormous amount of ice accumulates. Forced by the weight of the ice and the pull of gravity, these sheets of ice start moving, almost like a river, although most glaciers move no more than a couple of inches per day.

Skaftafell Glacier, Iceland

Layers of compacted ice make up a glacier

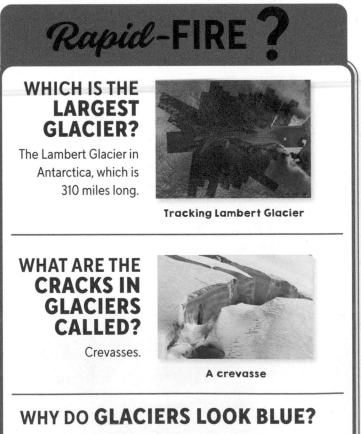

Big? HOW DO GLACIERS FORM?

In places high above the snow line, where more snow gathers than melts, it gets tightly packed. New snow falls and buries the old snow, which turns more dense and grainy. This is called firn and the process is called firnification. Layers of firn build up on top of each other, and as they get thick and heavy the grains of firn merge into huge masses of ice. Over time, the tightly compacted ice becomes so heavy and exerts so much pressure that the glacier slowly starts to move and slide downhill.

Rapid-FIRE?

WHICH IS THE LARGEST GLACIER?

The Lambert Glacier in Antarctica, which is 310 miles long.

Tracking Lambert Glacier

WHAT ARE THE CRACKS IN GLACIERS CALLED?

Crevasses.

A crevasse

WHY DO GLACIERS LOOK BLUE?

Ice absorbs red light; only the blue is reflected.

WHAT IS THE STUDY OF GLACIERS CALLED?

Glaciology.

WHAT ARE **FJORDS?**

Fjords are very deep, long and narrow inlets with steep sides or sheer cliffs, seen along the coasts of Norway, New Zealand, and Canada. A fjord is formed when the ocean comes in to fill the U-shaped valley left by a glacier after it has retreated.

Sunnylvsfjorden, Norway

WHY ARE **GLACIERS IMPORTANT?**

Glaciers are a very important source of fresh water. Melting glacier ice keeps many of Earth's rivers flowing. Glaciers create fertile valleys for farming, and their deposits are also rich in resources.

Arête
Cirque basin
Pyramidal peak
Tongue
Medial moraine
Terminal moraine

WHAT IS AN **ALPINE GLACIER?**

When they form in the high mountains, these rivers of ice are called alpine glaciers. They flow down through the mountains, cutting and breaking up the rocks, creating sharp peaks, ridges, and gouging out unique, U-shaped valleys.

Alpine glaciers

HOW DO **GLACIERS SHAPE LAND?**

The sheer weight and size of glaciers gives them an enormous power to carve out the landscape. Much like mega bulldozers, they crush and grind everything that gets in their way, pushing the debris along until it is deposited in distinctive piles called moraines.

Glacier damage on a rock face, and moraine deposits

WHAT ARE DESERTS?

Deserts are vast and extremely dry lands that receive very little or no rainfall. They can be both hot and cold—in both cases, the amount of evaporation is higher than the precipitation received, and the land remains very dry.

The Libyan Sahara

Big? WHY ARE DESERTS ARID?

Antarctic polar desert

Deserts are dry for different reasons depending on where they are. Winds in subtropical deserts, such as the Sahara in northern Africa, prevent rain clouds from forming. Coastal deserts, like the Atacama in Chile, get no rain, just a little moisture from fog. Death Valley in California, USA, is a rain shadow desert on mountainsides that face away from rain-filled winds. The Gobi, in Mongolia, is an interior desert; rain-bearing winds cannot reach so far inland. Polar deserts, such as the Arctic and Antarctic, are dry because the water is locked as ice.

HOW HOT OR COLD CAN A DESERT GET?

Deserts can have extremes in temperature. Daytime may get as hot as 129 °F in hot deserts, while at night, dryness and lack of cloud cover cause a sharp drop in temperature, and it can get as cold as 39 °F.

Death Valley, USA

Desert sand

WHERE DID THE SAND IN THE DESERT COME FROM?

Today's deserts were not always arid lands, and their soil was held in place by plants and trees. But when vegetation dies out, the soil is exposed to erosion. Gradually, the lighter clay and dried organic particles are blown away by the wind, leaving behind grains of sand made up of small particles from eroded rocks.

WHAT IS A SAND DUNE?

Sand dunes

When grains of sand pile up to form a mound or ridge, it is called a sand dune. Dunes are usually formed by wind blowing the sand in one direction. They can be various shapes and sizes, including crescents, stars, and long ridges called seifs.

WHICH IS THE WORLD'S YOUNGEST DESERT?

The Aralkum Desert, in Uzbekistan and Kazakhstan. It was once a water body called the Aral Sea, but water from the two rivers that fed it was diverted for agriculture and, gradually, by 2000, most of the sea had become a desert.

Rapid-FIRE **?**

CAN IT SNOW IN THE SAHARA?

Rarely, but yes!

Snowfall in the Sahara

WHAT IS AN OASIS?

An oasis is where water from a source deep underground comes to the surface in a desert, supporting life and vegetation.

Trees show an oasis

WHAT IS A WADI?

It is the Arabic name for a desert riverbed that fills when it rains.

Wadi Bani Khalid, Oman

HOW MUCH OF THE WORLD IS COVERED BY DESERTS?

A fifth of its entire land area.

Boats stranded in what was the Aral Sea

WHAT ARE CAVES?

Caves are natural hollows formed underground, usually large enough for a human to enter. Even if the entrance seems small and narrow, it may open up to be wider, or lead into deep underground passages. Most caves are formed over a long period of time by the gradual erosion of rock by water.

Gyokusendo Caves, Okinawa, Japan

Rapid-FIRE?

WHAT IS AN EXPERT ON CAVES CALLED?

A speleologist.

Exploring caves

HOW BIG IS THE SARAWAK CHAMBER IN BORNEO?

Big enough to fit around 40 747 airplanes inside!

Cave in Sarawak, Borneo

WHICH IS THE DEEPEST KNOWN CAVE?

Krubera Cave (also known as Voronja) in the Arabika Massif Mountain region of Georgia, which is 7,208 ft deep.

WHICH IS THE BIGGEST SINGLE CAVE?

Miao Room Cavern, beneath Ziyun Getu He Chuandong National Park, China.

WHAT ARE GLACIER CAVES?

Glacier caves, or ice caves, form inside a glacier as water enters through cracks and crevices in the ice. This water slowly melts and erodes the ice within the glacier, enlarging the cracks, sometimes creating long tunnels leading right down to its base.

Ice cave, Lake Baikal, Russia

DO CAVES SUPPORT ANY LIFE FORMS?

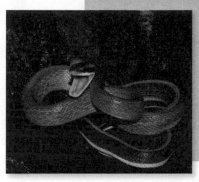

There are life forms, such as cave fish, that are specially adapted to life inside a cave. Some insects, salamanders, frogs, and snakes prefer life in a cave but can also live outside. Others animals like bats, bears, etc., use caves to shelter in.

Racer Snake, Thailand

Luray Caverns, USA

WHAT ARE STALACTITES AND STALAGMITES?

Over time, stalactites (icicle-shaped structures) form and hang from the roof, while on the cave floor the mineral deposits accumulate to form tall cones, called stalagmites.

WHAT IS A POLJE?

After a while, a cave may slowly corrode to such an extent that the roof is unable to withstand the weight of the soil above and collapses. The large hole in the ground that results is called a polje.

Big? HOW DO CAVES FORM?

A cave carved out by waves

The most widely seen caves are formed in limestone, dolomite, or rock gypsum. When it rains, rainwater and carbon dioxide in the air combine to form a mildly acidic solution, which seeps into the ground, dissolving the calcite in these rocks to create cavities underground. The crashing of waves against cliffs along a coastline also carves out caves. Caves can form in volcanic lava as the outer layer cools and hardens while the lava underneath continues to flow and drains away, leaving a hollow. Earthquakes can also crack rocks and create caves.

WHAT IS AN OXBOW LAKE?

When a river flows through low-lying plains, it slows down, carving out a meandering path with many U-shaped curves. Over time, some of these curves become cut off from the main flow of the river by the buildup of silt deposits, and form oxbow lakes. These distinctive, curved water bodies are close to a river but separate from it.

Oxbow lake on the Sava River, Croatia

WHAT IS A **WATERSHED?**

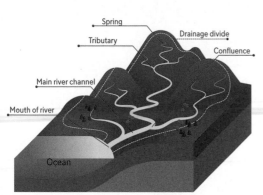

A river and its tributatries

A river can originate from the end of a melting glacier or snow. It can also start from a lake or a spring. As it flows downstream, the river is joined by many tributaries, which increase its flow to make one large river. The land area that feeds, or drains into, a specific river and its tributaries is the watershed for that river system.

HOW MANY TRIBUTARIES DOES THE NILE RIVER HAVE?

The Nile in Africa is the longest river in the world. The river has three tributaries; the two main ones are the White Nile that begins in Burundi and the Blue Nile that has its source in Ethiopia. Both rivers merge in Sudan. The third tributary, Atbara River, is dry most of the year and only flows if it rains in Ethiopia.

Big? HOW DO CANYONS FORM?

A canyon is an enormous, bounded valley with steep, rising sides. Canyons are formed by weathering and erosion. Over millions of years, the land is continuously worn away by water. Rocks and silt on the riverbed are carried away by the river, which further gouges out a narrow channel-shaped landscape.

Eroded sandstone at Antelope Canyon, Arizona, USA

Rapid-FIRE ?

HOW OLD IS THE NILE RIVER?

At least 30 million years old.

Nile River, Egypt

HOW OLD IS THE COLORADO RIVER?

At least 80 million years old.

Colorado River, USA

HOW MUCH WATER DOES THE AMAZON CARRY?

About one-fifth of all the Earth's river water.

HOW DO RIVER CURRENTS IMPACT THE LANDSCAPE?

Current refers to the speed of the movement of water. This can be very fast, especially in the mountains, close to the source of the river. River currents have tremendous power—they can tear out boulders and carry huge rocks and smash them deep into the riverbed. As the river reaches the plains, the current slows it down, causing it to deposit a lot of the debris it carried, creating a wider valley with fertile soil.

Raging waters of a fast-flowing river

Amazon River, South America

HOW DID THE AMAZON RIVER GET ITS NAME?

The Spanish soldiers who explored the region for the first time in 1541 battled native female warriors who fought bravely. The name the invaders gave to the river came from the Persian *hamazan*, meaning "those who fight together"—also used in Greek mythology for outstanding women warriors.

WHAT ARE THE NORTH AND SOUTH POLES LIKE?

In geographical terms, the North Pole is the northernmost point on Earth's axis of rotation. It is located in the Arctic, on the drifting, six to ten feet thick ice that covers the water of the ocean here. The warmest the North Pole gets is 32 °F. Usually, though, the temperature is below freezing, and bitterly cold. In summer, the North Pole is bathed in constant daylight; but the winter is a long, continuous dark night.

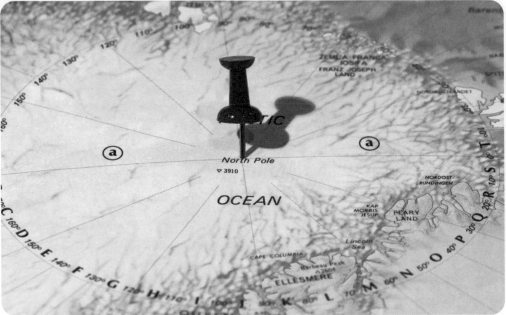

The geographic North Pole

DOES ANYONE LIVE AT THE NORTH POLE?

Drifting ice makes it very difficult to create settlements at the North Pole. It is an uninhabited area that does not belong to any nation. But it does have research stations based there to study the region and look for changes in the ecosystem.

Big?

WHAT ARE ICEBERGS AND WHY ARE THEY DANGEROUS?

Most of an iceberg remains under water

Icebergs are huge pieces of ice that break off glaciers and float into the ocean. They can be more than 15 feet in height, but most of their bulk remains submerged. Icebergs are dangerous. If a ship hits an iceberg, it can be badly damaged and sink. The most dangerous waters are in the North Atlantic, around Greenland, and in the Southern Hemisphere around Antarctica. Since 1912, after the luxury liner *Titanic* hit an iceberg and sank, the International Ice Patrol tracks icebergs and warns ships in the North Atlantic. Satellite data used to monitor icebergs, however, can only spot icebergs larger than 1,640 ft².

ARE ICE SHELVES COLLAPSING FASTER TODAY?

Yes, scientists have observed ice shelves falling much more rapidly now. What used to take months to break off is now collapsing in days. This is because the ice shelves of the Antarctic are experiencing warmer temperatures as part of a much wider climate change.

A free-floating chunk of an ice shelf

WHAT MAKES ANTARCTICA SO IMPORTANT FOR SCIENTISTS?

Antarctica, which is often termed as world's "largest natural laboratory," gives scientists the unique opportunity to study a region that has remained mostly unchanged by humans over millions of years. The various types of rocks and samples of ice taken from here have helped scientists make many discoveries, such as an explanation of ice ages.

Research station, Antarctica

Rapid-FIRE ?

Are the MAGNETIC AND THE GEOGRAPHIC NORTH POLES THE SAME?

No. The geographic North Pole is where longitudinal lines meet. Compasses indicate the magnetic North, which is not a fixed point.

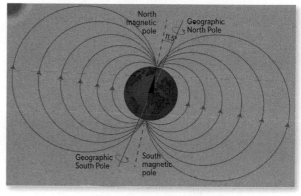

North magnetic pole

11.5°

Geographic North Pole

Geographic South Pole

South magnetic pole

The magnetic north and south

WHERE DO YOU FIND PENGUINS: THE ARCTIC OR THE ANTARCTIC?

Antarctic.

Penguins on ice

IS THERE ANY LAND AT THE NORTH POLE?

No, none. There is only ice.

WHAT ARE ICE SHELVES?

Mostly found in Antarctica, ice shelves are thick chunks of ice that float on the ocean while remaining connected to the coastline. They are formed when ice sheets float out from glaciers. The extreme cold prevents them from melting, and they accumulate as large floating blocks.

Ice shelf